Treasured Stories
of the
War Between The States

By Those Who Witnessed It

Dr. Tony Zeiss

Wake Forest, NC
www.scuppernongpress.com

Treasured Stories of the War Between The States By Those Who Witnessed It
Dr. Tony Zeiss

Copyright © 2024 Dr. Tony Zeiss

Second Printing

The Scuppernong Press
PO Box 1724
Wake Forest, NC 27588
www.scuppernongpress.com

Cover and book design by Frank B. Powell, III

All rights reserved.
Printed in the United States of America.

No part of this book may be reproduced or transmitted in any form or by any means, electronic or mechanical, including photocopying, recording, or by any information and storage and retrieval system, without written permission from the editor and/or publisher.

International Standard Book Number
ISBN 978-1-942806-66-0

Library of Congress Control Number: 2024939891

CONTENTS

Introduction 1
Judge Aston's Watch 3
"I Don't Know" 5
"Here, Chickee, Chickee" 7
"I Guess He's A Drinkin' Yet" 11
War Breeds Brutes 13
"I'm No Republican" 15
Glimpse Of History 19
"Goose Fishing" 21
"Family Grit" 23
"Death House" 25
"They Drowned My Grandfather" 27
"A Mighty Long Walk" 29
"Sherman's Men Took Everything" 31
"Mama, It's Me!" 33
"Broken Hearts" 35
"We Didn't Never Forget" 37
"I Ain't Ashamed Of It Neither" 39
"Best Woman In The World" 41
"The Mystery Is Solved" 43
"The Scallywag Skipped" 45
"Horrors Of The Prison Pen" 47
About The Author 51

INTRODUCTION

Each of the stories in this book originated from eye witnesses of the U. S. War Between the States and have been passed down through two, three, and sometimes four generations of family members. Every effort was made to insure historical accuracy, but specific facts regarding the incidents portrayed in these family gems were often sketchy and incomplete. The stories, however, are unique in their own right and worthy of preservation in print.

As each generation passes, the flavor and accuracy of such stories begin to diminish and eventually vanish or they tend to take on exaggerated, even mythical characteristics. In either situation, we lose a part of Americana, a part of the true picture of what life was like for the veterans and their families during that most trying time in our country's history. Printing these selected stories will hopefully contribute to the preservation of oral history and to our understanding of the men, women, and children who lived through that difficult historical period.

Most of my sources lived in the Carolinas and the primary theme their families remembered was the terrible way Union General Sherman's men decimated homes, farms, and businesses throughout Georgia and especially the Carolinas. However there are many stories presented from northern families as well. Humans have long family memories.

Collecting these stories from ordinary people throughout the country was a fascinating experience. My father intrigued my interest in this historical war by sharing stories from his grandfather who fought in it. In the 1980s I decided to search for additional stories and put them in book form. I visited retirement homes and churches, but casual conversations with friends and associates produced many stories. This book was so popular, especially with young people, that I continued collecting stories and had a second book, Authentic Stories of the War Between the States, published.

During this story-collecting process, I received one audio tape of an eye witness, met the niece of Confederate General Stephen Ramseur, and interviewed scores of people who were eager to share a part of their first-hand heritage from their grandfather or grandmother. To each of them we owe a debt of gratitude.

I have chosen to mostly use the title "War Between the States" as opposed to the "Civil War" because a civil war is between two or more factions of people fighting to determine who will govern a nation. The Southern states seceded and formed their own nation.

These treasured vignettes, often the only link between twenty-first century families and their ancestors who participated in the war, should be enjoyed by people who wish to catch a first-hand glimpse of that historic era. Through these stories, we can all witness the events that veterans and eye witnesses chose to recall and share with their loved ones. In a small way, we can feel what it must have been like to be there, experiencing some of the human challenges of Americans in the nineteenth century.

— *Tony Zeiss*

This Book Is Dedicated To A Great American Storyteller
— Robert E. Zeiss —

JUDGE ASTON'S WATCH
As told by Hubbard Sullivan

November 11, 1993

This story was told to Mr. Sullivan by Mr. Fred Hull in the year 1920. Mr. Hull was City Treasurer of Asheville, North Carolina and lived well into his nineties.

Mr. Hull, a native of Michigan, was encouraged to move to the mountains of North Carolina by a physician because of a recurring respiratory problem. He visited Asheville in 1885 and discovered it much to his liking. During this three or four-month summer visit, he attempted to befriend a prominent judge and Mayor in Asheville named Edward J. Aston. Judge Aston was slow to warm up to a "Damn Yankee" and never had anything remotely kind to say about people from the North. In fact, Judge Aston cursed the Yankees every time Mr. Hull would try to talk with him.

The primary source of Judge Aston's long-lived anger was an event that occurred in 1865 just at the end of the War. It seemed that a Michigan cavalry outfit was returning home from the hostilities and camped on the French Broad River some five miles south of Asheville. The Captain told his troops they could go into town and take about anything they wanted. One of the miscreants relieved the judge of his prized monographed gold pocket watch while the judge stood on the steps of the Buck Hotel. The judge, of course, never forgot this cowardly theft and thereafter condemned all Northerners as thieves and scalawags.

That autumn Mr. Hull returned to Michigan to gather his belongings and prepare to move permanently to Asheville. At a "going away" party, a neighbor asked Hull to deliver something for him and handed Hull a small box addressed to Judge Aston. After Hull returned to Asheville, he gave the package to the judge who opened it and was shocked to find his stolen gold watch. Needless to say, the grumpy judge was astonished. Mr. Hull said the revered Judge Aston never felt quite so badly toward him or the Yankees after that.

"I DON'T KNOW"
As told by Mrs. Paul Edu-Johnson (Lillian)

November 11, 1993

Mrs. Edu-Johnson's ancestors, the Connelys, were abolitionists and they took her father in when his parents died while he was just a boy. Her father, Smith Albert Posten, was just six or seven years old when a Confederate cavalry unit came through that part of West Virginia between Kingwood and Morgantown. The neighbors alerted each other about such raids so the men, women, and children who could drive livestock had time to hide the animals. They divided what horses, cattle, and pigs they had and drove them off in different directions to the woods. In this manner, the animals' footprints were scattered and it was less likely that all the livestock would be taken in the raid. Smith, being too young to take livestock to the woods, was left sitting on the slope of the front yard with instructions to answer every question from the confederate raiders with a simple, "I don't know."

In a little while some cavalrymen came down the road and inquired of Little Smith where his family was. "I DON'T KNOW," He firmly replied. This answer was repeated time after time to questions about their livestock, grain, and other things prized by the pillagers. Finally, and officer got off his horse and presented a lump of sugar, probably rock candy, to the boy. He tempted the boy with it for a long time. Smith had never seen a piece of candy look so good in his entire life. His family had not had any sugar for at least two years, but he held fast to his resolve.

At the end of the lengthy interview, the officer sat the boy on his lap and gave him one last try, encouraging him to tell where his family had gone with the livestock. Smith still "didn't know." The big Confederate then patted him on his head and said, "You are a loyal little boy and a credit to your people." He handed the lump of sugar to the boy and they rode off down the road.

Author's Note: Mrs. Edu-Johnson offered the following post script: "My Mother always said I shouldn't tell that story so often because it gives the South a good name."

"HERE, CHICKEE, CHICKEE"
As told by Robert Zeiss

A favorite story of the author's father, Robert Zeiss involved two colleagues of his maternal grandfather, Calvin Carey. Young Calvin was mustered into the 17th Indiana Light Artillery on December 4, 1863, just in time to fight with General Phillip Sheridan in the Shenandoah Valley Campaigns. He was mustered out to the service on July 8, 1865.

This event took place in the summer of 1864 in Virginia. It seems that two of Grandfather Carey's messmates elected to forage for some edibles beyond the usual hard tack (stale crackers) and sow belly (rancid bacon). Much to the concern of Calvin and their battery Captain, the two foragers did not return that day, nor the next, or even the day following. Finally, on the fourth day of their absence without leave, the two bedraggled soldiers stumbled back into camp. Upon fervent inquiry by their friends and after stuffing themselves with hard tack and coffee, the two comrades told their story.

The two young foragers began walking southward at the break of dawn hoping to locate a farmhouse that might favor them with a home-cooked meal. Short of this bounty, they reasoned that they would at the very least discover a patch of sweet potatoes or perhaps shoot a squirrel or two.

Somewhere near mid-morning, they occasioned upon a likely looking southern homestead. Although there were few, if any, animals around, the house and yard fence were in good repair, visible signs of prosperity. Two old roosters scratched in the dust. Boldly, the two northern soldiers advanced to the fence and called out. A house servant opened the squeaky door and answered their greeting. "Land o' mighty. Ain't you'uns Yankees?" she exclaimed.

"Why yes, ma'am, we are."

"What on God's earth are you doin' here?"

"Just hoping to find something to eat, ma'am" replied one of the soldiers. Having sympathy for the young boys and having a great admiration for President Lincoln, the woman gestured to the boys to hurry up to the porch.

"The missus is takin' a nap and she don't want no Yankees no how. Besides that, from the dust a-flyin' on the road, it appears some cav'ry are a comin'." The two surprised Yankees quickly assessed their situation and appealed to the black woman for help.

"Get under the porch here. Nobody will expect two Yankees to be under there." Without another word, they scrambled underneath the large front porch. It was dark and musty, but they reasoned a few minutes of discomfort wouldn't hurt. As the horsemen approached the house, it was obvious they were going to stop. The hidden foragers saw through the porch cracks that it was a rebel cavalry unit.

Much to the soldiers' disdain, they heard an officer tell his men to dismount and set up camp! Fortunately, the Yankees both had nearly full canteens, but what would they eat? How could they survive in such cramped and inhospitable surroundings? In very little time, Confederate "dog" tents were erected all around the front yard. There was no chance for escape. They would simply have to "tough it out." By sundown the two had become extremely hungry and the aroma of supper cooking on the Confederate's campfires didn't help at all. Then, the hungry stowaways heard the house servant step onto the porch.

"Here chickee. Here chickee," she began to call. In an instant, the two old roosters ran for the front porch as was their custom. With obvious accuracy, the woman began dropping rather large pieces of corn bread through the cracks in the porch. No one had to tell the two captives it was time to eat!

Of course they had to reach their share of cornbread before the roosters got it all.

Fortunately, their benefactor continued to feed those old roosters as often as she dared throughout the duration of the Confederate Cavalry's two day stay. By the time the two union artillerymen got back to their camp, hard tack and sow belly seemed to be food fit for kings!

"I GUESS HE'S A DRINKIN' YET"

As told on numerous occasions by Robert Zeiss

With my father and his brother, Richard sitting on his knees, Grandfather Carey would tell about the one and only time he was captured by the enemy. He and a close companion had ventured beyond their Union picket line foraging for their supper, a common practice in those latter days of the War Between the States when food provisions were scarce. The exact time and location of this event has been obscured by time, but it appears to have taken place in the Shenandoah Valley, Virginia, in the first part of August, 1864.

Much to their surprise, the two young recruits found themselves surrounded by a Confederate reconnaissance patrol. Recognizing that resistance would be futile, they surrendered their rifles and themselves to the mercy of their Union enemies. After a short discussion, it was determined that one Union private would be released from the patrol to deliver the two captives to the Captain of their main command located several miles south.

The ill-tempered guard tied their hands tightly in front and warned them that his rifle had a hair-trigger and he would happily dispose of them both to keep from having to make a hot trip for about ten miles back to the main camp.

"I'm authorize to shoot you for any attempts you make to escape!" Calvin and his friend believed he would do just that if he got the chance. They realized that there was no opportunity to escape because the guard was on a horse while they were on their feet.

After about two hours of walking on that hot August day, the captives and their guard suffered terribly from the heat and dust kicked up by wind gusts across the road. Naturally, Calvin and his friend began talking about finding a cool drink of water, as opposed to the tepid water in their canteens. As luck would have it, they came upon a spring of water under the shade of some trees next to the road.

It was difficult to determine at this moment which of two thoughts were uppermost in the prisoners' minds: thirst or escape. In any event, at the urging of the captives, their cranky guard finally agreed to stop for a drink of the cool water. A large wooden barrel had been sunk into the wet ground to provide clear, moss-free water to drink. A "dipper gourd" hung from a piece of twisted wire on a tree limb.

"Don't even think of doing anything stupid or I will shoot one of you and gut the other with my pig knife," snarled the guard.

Both the captives retrieved a long drink from the barrel and made great exclamations about the refreshing qualities of the experience. The guard decided that a drink of the cool liquid would be worth a slight risk. After motioning the captives away from the water barrel, he dismounted, grabbed the gourd, and leaned over to dip some water. At that moment, Calvin and his companion rushed the guard and grabbed a leg apiece. In unison, they lifted the guard's legs in a manner which pushed his body, head first, into the water barrel up to his waist.

At this precise spot in the story, Grandfather Carey would always lapse into silence. The imaginative and intensely interested grandsons would quickly exclaim, "What happened next, Grandfather? What happened next?"

"Well boys," Grandfather Carey would say with great seriousness and a twinkle in his eye, "I guess he's a drinkin" yet."

WAR BREEDS BRUTES
As told by Nelle Ferguson

June 12, 1994

Eliza Coleman, Mrs. Ferguson's Grandmother, was rearing at least three small children alone on their small farm in Hancock County, Tennessee during those dark days of the War Between the States. Her husband and all the menfolk were off fighting. One autumn day, Eliza got the word that the "Feds" were coming. They were raiding and pillaging and burning everything in sight. Eliza took the children with provisions and blankets and fled to the woods to hide.

Meanwhile, the Feds indeed came pillaging through the county. After a few days they left. Eliza and her children, weary and hungry from their time in the woods, returned to find their house ransacked as well as the barn and all the out buildings. Mrs. Ferguson said, "The children cried, especially because those soldiers had taken or destroyed all their playthings, including some colored beads the girls were so fond of. Those troops had smashed every one of the beads with stones." Eliza was heartsick about the children's things, but even more distressed by the fact that all of her dishes had been thrown against the walls and broken and they had taken all the food left in the house and barn. Eliza said "everything was a complete wreck."

The most horrendous thing, Eliza said, was the Feds had led Eliza's only horse up on the front porch and killed it. The huge animal, a pet to the children, lay there bloating in the warm sun. "She and the kids had an awful time getting that big old horse off the porch and away from the house," Mrs. Ferguson related. "But she was always happy they hadn't burned the house!"

"I'M NO REPUBLICAN"
From the records of Elbert Franklin Brown, Great-grandfather of F. Beth Foley Zeiss

Young Frank Brown enrolled in the 1st Tennessee Regiment commanded by Col. Peter Turney in May, 1861. Frank fought in many battles and skirmishes with this regiment both as a scout in Company E, commanded by Captain Davis, and later as a lieutenant in the cavalry in the 23rd Newman's battalion. He was wounded in the right jaw by a grape shot early in his service to his country somewhere in Virginia. This caused a three month separation from military service, but he returned to fight until paroled at Guntersville, Alabama on May 17, 1865. He was paroled and took the required oath of allegiance to the U.S. Government "in order to be allowed to go home unmolested or restricted."

The 1st Tennessee Regiment began with 1,250 men and, with additional recruits over four years, had a grand total of 3,200 men. Only 65 were paroled at the end of the war according to the memoirs of Sam Watkins, author of *Co. Aytch* of the 1st Tennessee. Many of these men had been separated from the original regiment, as was Mr. Brown, but many were killed or wounded in places like Manassas, Chickamauga, Perryville, and Franklin, Tennessee.

The twenty-eight-year old Brown suffered from his facial wound and from severe kidney trouble. He was often separated from his unit during forced marches because his kidneys would pain him so much when riding his horse. He was left to find his own way as best he could, whenever he could get there.

After the war, his health failed and he and his wife and three daughters scratched out a living on 46 acres, worth an estimated $100, a house worth $75, and two cows of undetermined worth.

He was appointed as Moore County Clerk and that income really helped. Nonetheless, Frank was much encouraged in 1899 when the State of Tennessee established a pension fund for its glorious sons of the late war. Imagine his disgust and frustration when he was refused the pension time and again because of insufficient proof that he had served his state or that he had been wounded.

Over the next five years, several of his comrades, commanding officers, and attending physicians vouched for him to the pension board. Finally, he was awarded a pension, but it lasted only a few months because someone accused Mr. Brown of being a Republican! Of course, no self-respecting Southerner could expect any public pension from the great state of Tennessee if he were a Lincoln Republican — not even thirty-nine years after the war. Mr. Brown's pension was revoked.

Poor Frank, now around 65 years old, had not been able to work for five years because of cancer from his facial wound, continuous kidney trouble, and two troublesome legs which had been broken sometime after the war. Finally in desperation, he wrote the only person whom he thought could have any influence over the pension board — the board chairman's' wife, Mrs. Frank Moses. In brief form, his letter dated February 4, 1904 reads:

> *I write to you to ask a favor by way of years of influence with your husband. I am an old Confederate soldier who belonged to the 1st company and regiment that was reported to the Governor and to the Confederate authorities. I am now old and cannot work anymore and the doctor says I have cancer on my face, and that if I am ever to get what I am justly entitled to, I want it while I am living.*

I am no more a Republican that poor Peter Turney was a horse thief, neither am I a socialist! I am just simply a democrat from top to toes, and any man or set of men that have stated otherwise, is simply a fool and a liar besides.

Now say to your partner, Mr. Moses, if they are determined that I shall not be reinstated on the role of honor, I will immediately ask the board to drop my name from the role, then I will not stand in the eyes of the people of the state as a perjured man. Respectfully, I am E. F. Brown, a wronged old soldier.

Frank's strategy worked. Shortly afterward he received his pension and kept it until his death. Unfortunately, his widow had to prove his case again to the pension board so she could continue receiving his pension as his widow.

GLIMPSE OF HISTORY
As told by Mrs. Frances R. Reville

November 11, 1993

Mrs. ReVille's grandfather, Ivey Redick (Reddick) joined the Confederate army early in the war and served as a volunteer, then later as a conscript (draftee). He served as 5th Corporal in McIntosh's Artillery Battery, often called the PEE DEE artillery in the Army of Northern Virginia.

At the Battle of Chancellorsville in May, 1863, Ivey was fighting with General Stonewall Jackson's command against the surprised troops of General Joseph Hooker. During the height of the battle, Ivey was hit in the stomach by a projectile which knocked him off a high ridge and sent him rolling over again and again to the bottom of a ravine.

General Jackson witnessed this event and exclaimed, "There goes Ivey boys, run down and get him. I think he's gone boys, I think he's gone!" But Ivey, unhurt except for bruises, jumped up and yelled that he was okay. (He must have been hit by a spent shell of some kind.)

Ivey Redick fought to the end of the war, but was always angered by the fact that his fourteen-year-old brother hadn't joined the army with him. Ivey tried talking his brother into helping the Southern cause, but the boy refused. Ivey became furious about his brother's refusal and changed his name to Redick with only one "d" and never spoke to his brother again.

Author's note: Mrs. ReVille, Ivey's Granddaughter, added when she was five or six-years-old, she often sat with her grandfather and listened to his war stories, but most, except this one, had faded from her memory. "However," Mrs. ReVille noted, "I witnessed several Confederate reunions where the old veterans would gather at one end of the front porch to recall events of the war while their sons would gather at the other end to discuss events of their day. The old veteran's sons didn't like to hear those same old stories from their fathers. We children played in the yard and the women generally stayed in the house, cooking mostly."

"GOOSE FISHING"
As told by Dr. Ted Gasper

March, 1995

Dr. Gasper's Grandmother, Susan "Sue Ida" Bouknight often told him this curious story about her father Daniel Pinckney Bouknight, a South Carolinian veteran of the War Between the States.

Young Daniel's South Carolina unit was, like most military outfits toward the end of the war, facing scarce provisions including weapons, ammunition, clothing, and especially food. Sometime in the spring of 1865, about the time Sherman's men were marching through the state, Daniel and his three mess mates developed a powerful appetite for meat. Hard tack and chicory coffee was in short supply and they had seen no meat for weeks.

The twenty-year-old Daniel and his friends were even forced to drink "Confederate Coffee," a starchy concoction made from dried bits of cut up potatoes. They longed for real coffee, but it was meat they most missed and most needed.

The boys were bivouacked somewhere in the deep south awaiting orders when they resolved to have meat at their next evening meal, no matter what might befall them. Certainly they were reluctant to forage (officers called it stealing) from the people they were defending, besides the locals were about as destitute as the soldiers. Nevertheless, their emaciated conditions and strong craving for meat overruled their civil consciences.

Early the next morning, the four messmates "borrowed" a company horse and proceeded to visit a barnyard they had marched by that morning a few miles back down the road. One of the boys artfully bent a small, but needle-sharp hat pin in the general shape of a fish hook. This instrument was tied to a twenty or thirty foot piece of twine and "baited" with a small piece of a shiny green Magnolia leaf.

Upon arriving at the unsuspecting farm, three of the boys hid behind a rail fence to watch the fourth comrade ride the horse on a slow walk into the barnyard with the twine tied to the saddle horn at one end and trailing behind the horse at the other. Immediately, a large sentinel goose announced the presence of the intruders with great vocal fanfare. The goose's attention, however, was quickly diverted by the darting, flashing Magnolia leaf bouncing across the ground much like a large, hopping beetle.

The goose became so determined to catch an easy meal, he snatched the homemade lure with the very first peck. Daniel's mess mate whipped the horse with a dangling rein causing it to leap forward, thereby securely hooking the goose through its bill.

Honking hoarsely with outstretched neck, the doomed goose had no choice, but to run after the horse to keep from being dragged to death. Alarmed by all the commotion, a matronly woman rushed out of the nearby farm house and hollered: "Lordy, Lordy mister, don't run so, he won't bite!"

Daniel and his friends enjoyed their dinner with much relish that evening.

"FAMILY GRIT"
As told by Hubbard Sullivan

November 11, 1993

Mr. Sullivan's great-grandfather, John Foard, was bedridden from a stroke at his home located across the south fork of the Yadkin River on the Rowan and Davies county line in North Carolina when Sherman's troops came through. Mr. Foard's daughter, Mary Owens, had come to nurse him and help out the house servants, old Tom and his wife. Mary had just lost her husband who had been a courier for General Lee and was shot from his horse and killed.

Mary and the servants were in a great state of anxiety because they could not remove her father to seek refuge from the invading troops. Mr. Foard told his daughter and servants to leave, but they remained steadfast, waiting for the worst. They didn't have long to wait.

As the Federal troops came through that country, they found a keg of brandy. No time was lost as the pillagers drank themselves into a high state of inebriation. Then they ransacked the small village and confiscated all the salt and sugar they could find. What they didn't keep, they spread all over the street so none of the local residents could use it. Next, they went from house to house terrorizing and stealing valuables from people.

The Yankees barged into the Foard house knocking about looking for anything to steal. When they came to Mr. Foard's closed door, they demanded that he come out. He refused. Then they began calling him an "old hypocrite" and worse. They thought he was just afraid of them. Finally, they gave him an ultimatum to come out or they would come in and make him come out. With this pronouncement, Mr. Foard told his daughter to hand him his rifle and to hide under the bed. He then shouted. "This gun's only got one shot, but the first one through the door get it!" After some silence and much to Mr. Foard's surprise, the soldiers retreated … but only to harass the servant, Tom.

The Yankees took the faithful servant and dragged him out to the front yard. After repeated, but unsuccessful attempts to get old Tom to tell where the family silverware and money had been hidden, they strung the poor man up by his thumbs to a high Oak limb and beat him until he lost consciousness. Tom never told them where the valuables were buried.

With this, the soldiers left to seek better luck and young Mary, along with Tom's wife, ran out and cut down old Tom. They eventually nursed Tom back to full consciousness and calmed Mr. Foard down. Tom and his wife lived the rest of their lives with the Foard family.

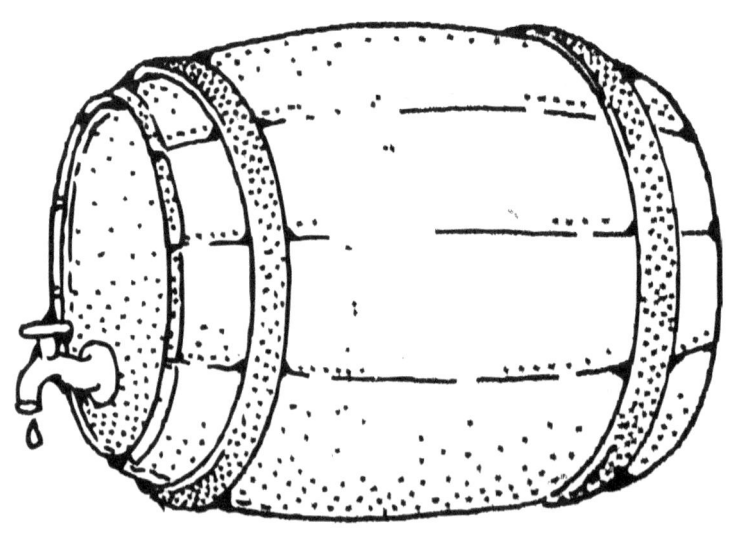

"DEATH HOUSE"
As told by Dee Zeiss

March, 1994

Billy Williams, Mrs. Zeiss's great grandfather from Ohio, joined a Union infantry outfit and was eventually assigned to a hospital unit, probably at a prisoner of war camp. Among other duties, he took his turn guarding the "death house," a common name for the makeshift morgue which held the bodies of poor dead soldiers until burial details could prepare them for shipment home or burial on site.

In those days, it was not uncommon for a soldier to be declared dead, only to revive later in the "death house" and live to a ripe old age. The surgeons, few in number and terribly overworked, could easily mistake a comatose soldier for a dead soldier. In fact, such mistakes occurred enough that the nurses and orderlies began tying small bells to a toe or finger on the bodies. The death house guard's responsibility was to simply listen for a bell to ring which meant someone was probably still alive. The guard would announce the news to the nearest nurse or surgeon and a rescue would be eminent.

On one particular dark evening, young private Billy Williams was almost asleep, sitting on a tree stump near the death house at the edge of the hospital grounds. As the midnight clouds covered the moon and stillness fell like a blanket over the compound, Billy heard a faint jingle. He dismissed it as his imagination, but then heard a distinct jingle followed by bell after bell, jingling amid a series of thumps inside the lamp less death house.

No one had to tell Billy to get up off his stump and seek help. As Mrs. Zeiss' Grandma would later relate, Billy wasted no time retrieving help along with some candle lanterns. Close inspection revealed *rigor mortis* or an involuntary muscle response of some sort triggered a chain reaction among the bodies stacked on top of each other resulting in two or three bodies falling or shifting to the hard plank floor. All were still dead for sure … but Billy stayed wide awake 'till morning!

"THEY DROWNED MY GRANDFATHER"

As told by John Montgomery Belk

Circa 2001

"Sherman's troops drowned my Grandfather, Abel Belk, down there at Gill's Creek located a short distance from his father Tom Belk's home. Abel lived in the Waxhaw community boarding the North and South Carolina border. Those Yankees were combing the countryside for anything they could steal, plunder, or burn. The South had mostly given up and there was no protection for anyone. Grandfather and a neighbor fled from their homes hoping the raiders would follow them and not destroy their homes or steal their property. After running some distance from their homes, the two neighbors hid near Gill's creek.

The Yankees soon found my grandfather and his neighbor and speculated that since they were able-bodied men and were not in the Confederate Army, they must be involved with the barrels of gold that were rumored to be hidden in the area. Of course, they were just farmers and there was no gold in the immediate area. (Reed's gold mine, located about 40 miles north was founded in the 1830s and the first U.S. Mint was established in Charlotte which probably prompted the Yankee speculation about gold.)

Sherman's troops were mostly unsupervised so they dragged my grandfather and his neighbor into the creek and pushed them under at gun point to try to get them to tell where the gold was. Each time the Yankees would lift them up for air, my grandfather and his neighbor would emphasize they were farmers and knew nothing about any gold. Finally, those Feds drowned them both.

Dr. Tony Zeiss

The neighbor's wife sent a letter to my grandmother telling her what had happened and that she had a wagon, but the Yankees had taken her horses. She suggested that if my grandmother had any horses, her farm hand would bring them back and they would retrieve the bodies for proper burial. Grandmother and the horses went over to the neighbors' farm, hooked up the wagon, and the two ladies and farm hand retrieved their husbands' bodies.

This sad incident left my grandmother a widow with three young sons to manage their small farm. Two and a half year-old William Henry, my father, was one of the three children."

Author's Note: I gave my condolences to my good friend, John Belk. At this time, John was President and CEO of Belk Department stores which existed all over the southern United States. His father, William Henry established the Belk stores. John, a historian in his own right, replied his family had not forgotten the tragedy and that Belk stores never celebrated or had sales on Decoration Day, now known as Memorial Day, because it was at first a Yankee holiday!

"A MIGHTY LONG WALK"
As told by Richard F. Green

November, 1993

    Mr. Green related this story about his Grandfather, William G. Clements, whom he well remembered.

Twenty-one-year-old farm laborer, Bill Clements volunteered with the 6th North Carolina Regiment in 1861, just in time to fight in the first major battle of that costly war. On July 21, 1861 the battle of Bull Run (Manassas), 25 miles Southwest of Washington City, was fought with two ill-prepared armies. Both armies were confident that the engagement would end the war quickly. They were wrong.

    At the end of the engagement, the Federals had nearly 2,000 men killed, wounded, or missing and the Confederates lost nearly 2,000 men in the same categories. Bill Clements was one of those southern casualties, having been wounded twice during the confused fighting on that horrible day.

    There were no field hospitals and the unfortunate wounded were simply carried by ambulance wagon or any other means to a holding place behind the lines. The wounded or killed southern troops were mostly transported to Manassas Junction. If the wounded made it alive through the trip to the Junction, they had a fair chance of surviving. Bill Clements managed to survive by washing his wounds in Bull Run Creek and stopping the bleeding by using moss from a tree's bark. His wounds were so serious, however, that he was sent home to North Carolina permanently.

    Twelve months later, Bill felt he had regained enough health to join his old regiment in the field. He caught up with the old outfit just in time to march under the command of General

Robert E. Lee to the sleepy little town of Sharpsburg, Maryland. In short order, Bill found himself preparing for a major battle at Antietam Creek on September 17, 1862. This engagement, even more terrible than Manassas, left more than 23,000 soldiers killed, wounded, or missing. It is considered to have been the bloodiest day of the entire war.

Bill escaped harm during the conflagration, but was hit by a Minnie ball as his regiment withdrew toward Shepherdstown. The lead missile shattered his left arm just below the elbow. After a torturous walk to find help, Bill suffered from the cold steel of a surgeon's knife and saw. He lost his arm and his ability to serve his country any longer as a soldier.

Just two days later, Bill set off in a southerly direction with nothing but the clothes on his person, a canteen full of creek water, and presumably, a few edibles. He hoped to catch a ride on the rails, but was never successful. With his fresh amputation and almost no provisions, Bill spent the next several weeks walking all alone, back to Morrisville, North Carolina, a journey of approximately 500 miles! As Bill told his children and grandchildren about that event, he would end by saying, "It was a mighty long walk!"

Author's Note: Bill lived to be eighty-four years old, became a respected leader in the Christian Church, and was superintendent of schools in Wake County, North Carolina. He obviously never developed an aversion for walking because he often walked to each school in Wake County to visit.

"SHERMAN'S MEN TOOK EVERYTHING"
As told by Sam Durrance

July, 1994

Mr. Durrance was often told this story by his maternal grandmother when he was a child. His Grandmother, Susannah Tyson Feagin, nee Fitch, witnessed the trials of war first hand when she was a child and she never got over it. Her Father was a scout in the Confederate Army and she, along with her brothers, sisters, and Mother, were alone for long periods at a time during that awful war. It seemed Susannah was most interested that her grandson also remember the terrible things Sherman's men did when they came through their part of South Carolina during that infamous march through Georgia and the Carolinas.

Shortly after Sherman's Federal Army captured Atlanta, the general ordered his men to march across Georgia to the Atlantic Ocean, then north through Columbia, South Carolina and up to the Raleigh-Hillsboro, North Carolina area. The intent of the march was to break the will of the beleaguered Southern people by destroying and ravaging everything, including the people in their path. The Southern families were defenseless. Most of the men were off in the military and the women, children, and old folks were left destitute for food and shelter.

When the news of the advancing army reached Susannah's mother in February, 1865, she and her children buried the family keepsakes and silverware. They also hid as much nonperishable food as possible. Meanwhile, Mrs. Fitch sent Susannah's eleven-year-old brother to a nearby swamp to hide their only cow.

The Federal army and a considerable number of camp followers spent three days in and around the Fitch farm killing and eating all the hogs and chickens except on old rooster, who refused to be caught, and twelve baby chicks. Even the family's only mule was expropriated without compensation.

Finally, the soldiers left the region and Susannah's brother came home after three days in the swamp with nothing, but mosquitoes, snakes, and the family cow for company. Sherman's men took everything!" was the common exclamation in those days. Interestingly, the old rooster raised the baby chicks just as a mother hen would.

Author's Note: It was just a few months later when the sad new reached Susannah and her family. First, they learned General Lee had surrendered at Appomattox Court House in southern Virginia. Shortly after that, they learned Susannah's father had been accidentally killed by Confederate sharpshooters as he attempted to return to camp on evening after scouting behind enemy lines.

"MAMA, IT'S ME!"
As told by Mrs. Bronce L. Ray

Mrs. Ray's father, Phillip A. Willis, was just a small curly-headed child of six or seven years old in 1862 when he contracted small pox. He was immediately moved into a quarantined hospital room in his home town of New Bern, North Carolina. His mother adored him and was heartbroken by their unavoidable separation. Visits were seldom allowed and even then, his mother could only look at him through a door from outside the room.

To make matters worse, a few weeks later a federal amphibious foray, commanded by Flag Officer Louis Goldsborough and Brigadier General Ambrose Burnside, attacked the harbor area and an earthen fort just below the city. This attempt to stop Confederate blockade runners by capturing their ports was pretty successful. The ships sent mortar shells screaming into the fort with much destruction. Young Phil and his fellow convalescents were made to hide under their beds throughout the bombardments.

Not long after this terrifying experience, Phil was released from the hospital and told to go home. Of course his face was disfigured from the pox scars and the nurses had cut off his beautiful curls in order to administer medicine. Of course, Phil was excited about his release and ran along the street toward home when he saw his loving mother coming toward him. He stopped to receive what he knew would be a joyous greeting, but his mother walked right past him.

"Mama, it's me!" Phil hollered. Mrs. Willis stopped, turned and was horrified to see what the small pox had done to her precious little boy.

Authors Note: Mrs. Ray ended this sad story by mentioning that her father "forever after thought Phil was ugly, but by the time I was a child, the pox marks had faded and he was a handsome man."

"Broken Hearts"
As told by Donna Sparkman

October 12, 1994

This sad story was told to Donna Sparkman by her mother-in-law, Hazel Brown Sparkman, granddaughter of Addie Mary Allock, "Mollie."

Mrs. Allock's father, "Tip" Allock, fought for the Confederacy until 1865 when news of the war's end reached his unit, then stationed in Mississippi. As was so often the case during those confusing days, Tip Allock was unable to find any means of transportation home to Western Kentucky beyond his own two feet.

With a rifle, bullet mold, and canteen as his only significant possessions, Tip walked the distance over several weeks. After being away from home for nearly nine months, Tip was no doubt thinking about the comforts of home, about a joyous reunion with his lovely bride, and about seeing his first child who should soon be born. These thoughts of home surely compelled him to keep putting one foot in front of the other day after long day, most of which brought much pain and hunger.

Tip finally reached his home county and quickened his pace. Just as his little hometown came into view, he noticed some men digging a grave in the cemetery on the outskirts of town. He recognized the grave diggers and asked them whose grave they were digging. With ashen faces they replied, "Why it's your wife's, Tip."

Tip rushed to his house in town and found his wife dressed out for burial. He was told some local Yankees had shown his wife a Confederate cap with a bullet hole through it and alleged it belonged to her husband. (Kentucky was a border state and produced both Yankees and Rebels, often from the same hometown or families). Her family told Tip that his young wife immediately took to her bed and gave birth to their daughter, and died shortly after her conversation with the Yankees. "It was a broken heart," they said.

Tip was introduced to his newly born baby daughter, "Mollie," by his widowed mother. A short while later he decided to purchase a piece of land in Arkansas to get away from the bad memories associated with his home town. Before moving his mother and daughter there, he drove a flock of domestic turkeys to his new home by foot. While returning to Kentucky for his mother and daughter, he took sick suddenly and died. His family claimed it was another case of a "broken heart."

Author's Note: Mrs. Sparkman suggested Mrs. Allock may have died from child birth complications and Mr. Allock from pneumonia, but family firmly believed it was heartbreak which killed their loved ones.

"WE DIDN'T NEVER FORGET"

As told by Hannah Norris Walker to her daughter Maxine Short
(tape recorded circa 1951)

Mrs. Short tape-recorded her mother's recollection of her war experience in the early 1950s. Her mother lived to be 97 years old, but never forgot one fateful day during the war when she was only three or four years old. This story is taken directly from the recording of this eye witness to history.

"My daddy didn't go in the fightin'. He stayed in the big cave (near Green Forrest, Arkansas) and made boots and shoes for them that's a fightin'. He was a regular shoemaker. He'd make 'em just as perty as the money could buy and he made boots for some of 'em that would come up to their hips."

Little Hannah's father was off working and living in the cave when the "Feds" assailed their house in the country.

"I was three years old when they came back and burned my mother and daddy's house. It was the Feds, we called them. Them old men was a tearin' the floor up, huntin' under it to see what we had under here. And one of them come in and got into my grandmother's big chest and pulled out a piece of her underwear. He put it on and danced with it out in the yard.

One of the men said to my mother, 'You better get your things out of here. We're gonna burn your house down.' My mother and oldest sister and brother began to pile things up and carry them away out to the grove of trees on the hill. As they began to burn the house, one of the men told my sister,

'You better get you lamb outa here, Sis, or it'll get burnt up.' And they all laughed about that remark.

We all then went to the grove of trees and watched. I remember just sittin' way out there and watchin' it burn and all of us was just worried to death. After that, my mother and us children had to live in an old stable, but I can't remember how long. It had a shelter over it and they cleaned it out and we lived in there and made out some way 'till they (family) came and got us.

It was meanness I reckon (that made them burn the house). They done everybody the same way. Now after the war was over, there's three of them men in that bunch that burned our house, that come back home and lived close to us. Yes sir. One of 'em lived within a mile and the other two lived about a mile away."

Upon this pronouncement, Hannah's daughter asked her if those neighbors were ever sorry about burning their house. "Well, they didn't ever say nothing about it, but we didn't try to harm them in any way. We just got by with them the best we could … but we didn't never forget what they done."

"I AIN'T ASHAMED OF IT NEITHER"

As told by Mr. Francis Thompkins

July 1984

As a young man, Mr. Thompkins, from Texas, witnessed the effects of the War Between the States even though he wasn't born until the late 1890s. He prefaced the story with the remark that "War made brutes of men. They'd all lost friends and property in that war, you see."

Mr. Thompkins remembered a neighbor who walked with a limp from a war wound. The veteran took a liking to the young Mr. Thompkins and shared one of his war exploits with him. Tompkins said he was always interested in that war, but "none of them old fellows talked too much about it."

However, his veteran friend did share this story around 1905. The Confederate veteran's infantry company got into a skirmish with some Yankee cavalry near a farm house somewhere over in Georgia. The Yankees were holed up in the woods just behind a barn and a hog lot. The rifle firing got pretty hot for a moment, but the Confederates finally pushed them from the woods and they skedaddled on their horses.

The victors found four dead Yankees lying in the woods and concluded that "it would be most expeditious to toss 'em into the hog lot" and let the hogs dispose of the bodies." Besides, they didn't have shovels or the time to bury them. The old veteran then told Tompkins, "and I ain't ashamed of it neither."

"BEST WOMAN IN THE WORLD"

Taken from *Recollections of a Confederate Soldier* by Edwin Calhoun, Provided by his great-nephew Mo Wright

July, 1994

Three cousins from South Carolina joined the Confederate cause in April, 1861 by enrolling in the 6th South Carolina Cavalry. Edwin, John and Frank Calhoun served together, fought together, and held their mess together wherever they went during the War Between the States. Another member of their cooking mess was "Dad" Donnelly, son of an esteemed preacher from their hometown.

Edwin Calhoun had married Sallie Tilman from Monterey, South Carolina just before the war broke out. Fortunately, her family and Edwin's family were rather well off. Edwin often sent Mike, his black attendant, back home to Sallie for boxes of staples. In Edwin's words: "We lived well generally. We had plenty of beef and bread, and could frequently get potatoes, chicken and, in winter, oysters. But if at any time our supplies became low, I would send Mike home and Sallie would send me a well-filled basket or box including a bottle or two of good old peach brandy which we enjoyed very much, especially "Dad."

Once I sent Mike home for a box and wrote a note asking for a bag of peas along with the usual food she included. In about two weeks, I was on picket duty when Mike returned to camp with the new box of food stuff. When I got off picket duty, I found "Dad" sitting by our campfire with his head resting back against a tree. I asked him if he were sick. The answer was 'no.' I then asked whether the box had come. 'Yes,' he replied. After a pause and without raising his head, he muttered. 'The box ain't worth a damn. Not a drop of brandy in it.'

In the box I found a cooked turkey, a large ham, some sausage, ribs, butter, light bread, cake and the bag of peas, but no brandy. About a week later to our great surprise and joy, we found that Sallie had put the brandy in the bag of peas. After ole Dad took his first drink of the brandy, he pronounced, 'Well, boys, I think Sallie is the best woman in the world.'"

"THE MYSTERY IS SOLVED"
As told by Martha Farmer

November 11, 1993

In 1862, Mrs. Farmer's grandfather, Henry Bryant, volunteered to serve in a North Carolina Regiment assigned to build defenses for the State. At one point, he was bivouacked with his unit just south of Charlotte. There was an inland naval yard and a coinage mint in Charlotte. It is speculated that Henry's unit was assigned to build earthen works in anticipation of an attack. In any event, young Henry spent several long months in this fairly isolated post doing nothing more than digging dirt defenses for the infantry to hide behind in the unlikely event they were attacked.

    Occasionally, they were given furlough to participate in dances held for the troops by the local citizens, consisting of many young ladies. At one of these activities, Henry fell deeply enamored with 16-year-old Julia Parks. But in the spring of 1863, just as Army life seemed to be getting more interesting for Henry, his unit was sent north on a campaign with General Robert E. Lee. Henry asked Julia to wait for him as he marched north up the muddy road with his unit.

    Henry pined for Julia, but found himself especially distracted in early July when the huge battle of Gettysburg erupted. Sometime during that two day holocaust, Henry was deeply punctured by something in the calf of his left leg. His wound produced much pain and fever and he could not walk for days. Nevertheless, Henry never sought a surgeon's help since army surgeons were notorious for removing limbs from wounded soldiers. Henry was curious about whatever was still inside his leg, but his greater concern was to remain whole for Julia. Months later, Henry, festering leg wound and all, mustered out of the Army and headed straight back to North Carolina to find his beloved Julia. Sure enough, Julia was still waiting for him and they were married shortly after she turned seventeen.

For the next fifteen years, Julia helped Henry dress his open wound every day. The draining wound was a constant reminder of that awful battle, but it also stirred much discussion about what kind of missile made the wound. Was it a piece of grape shot, buck and ball, shrapnel, or a Minnie ball?

As luck would have it, Henry, now thirty-five-years old, was riding in a hack (horse drawn bus) to church with his family, eight boys and a girl, when the horses were spooked. The animals jumped unexpectedly, knocking Henry from the vehicle. He felt his leg pop and something fell out of that old nagging wound.

"Julia, Julia, "he cried. "The mystery is solved. It's a Minnie Ball," Henry exclaimed as he held up the piece of lead.

Author's Note: "His leg then healed," said Mrs. Farmer, "and he had no more trouble with it. You can still see some of the earthworks he and those boys dug down there near Highway 521 below Pineville."

"THE SCALLYWAG SKIPPED"

As told by Edwin W. Berlin

June 16, 1994

Twenty-two-year-old James Monroe Berlin, later the grandfather of Edwin Berlin, had just begun an enterprising business career in Pennsylvania when the war broke out. President Lincoln only asked for 75,000 volunteers to combat what he called the rebellion. Almost no one on either side thought there would really be all-out war and the idea that it might last longer than three months was beyond comprehension. The conflict escalated, however, and by the time the first battle of Manassas (Bull Run) was over, it was clear more Northern troops were needed. Mr. Lincoln repeatedly put out the call for more troops and by 1862 Congress passed a conscription law which drafted men for the army. Generally every able-bodied man between the ages of 18 and 40 was required to join the war effort.

There were two basic exceptions to conscription. One, a conscript could pay $300, a hefty sum in those days, for an exemption, but he would again be eligible when the next draft occurred. The second exception went into effect if the conscript could find someone else to stand in for him and serve his allotted term, usually three years at this time.

Jim Berlin decided to use all of his financial resources to avoid his stint in the war by paying a "stand in" $300 to serve in the army in his place. Unfortunately, the "Scallywag skipped" and was never heard from again.

Poor Jim was summarily "volunteered" for three full years of active duty. He was mustered into Company C, 5th Regiment Artillery of the New York Volunteers on February 11, 1862. His unit saw action throughout the Shenandoah Valley campaign with General Sheridan. He fought at Fisher's Hill, New Market, and in other battles during his tenure in Mr. Lincoln's army.

"HORRORS OF THE PRISON PEN"

Taken from a narrative written by Aaron Eugene Bachman, a Union Veteran as presented by a descendant, Mark T. Bachman

Shortly after his eighteenth birthday, Eugene Bachman, an apprenticed blacksmith, enlisted in Company L, 1st Pennsylvania Cavalry. Eugene was large for a cavalry man, weighing nearly two hundred pounds and standing at six feet tall. His blacksmith skills were highly valued, particularly since he could make a hundred horse shoes in only seven hours. He still rode horses like everyone else in his unit, but he was too large to be selected for any scouting or courier duty.

During his three years and ten months of service, Eugene saw battle several times, spent months in hospitals recuperating from "swamp fever," an infectious disease transmitted by horses to humans, and suffered from poor diet. Like most men on both sides of the war, Eugene experienced disagreeable and unhealthy conditions. His experience as a prisoner of war, however, made everything else pale by comparison.

In November, 1863, Eugene's Cavalry unit engaged the enemy near Culpepper Court House, Virginia. His horse threw a front shoe while crossing a corduroy culvert (made of small limbs) and became lame by nightfall. He asked to be excused from duty for the following day, but every man was needed as they faced the Confederates at New Hope Church. Unfortunately, Eugene's horse could not outrun a group of Confederate Cavalry officers and he was captured.

Eugene was first taken to Libby prison in Richmond, Virginia which packed hundreds of men into a large tobacco warehouse. He was then moved to Belle Island, on the James River at Richmond for several months where they lived mostly with no facilities. Then he was transferred to even worse conditions at the dreaded Andersonville prison in Georgia.

From March through September, poor Eugene endured sickness, starvation, filth, blistering heat, thirst, and abuse along with thousands of other unfortunate Union prisoners trying to stay alive on that bare hillside. The open prison offered nothing to shelter them from the elements and scarcely enough water in a small stream to sustain the lives of the prisoners. Eugene described human behavior at its worst when Confederate guards killed anyone who stepped too close to the "dead line" or when a prisoner committed some other infraction of the rules. The "dead line" stretched 19 feet along the inside of the log wall. This line was designed to prevent prisoners from climbing or tunneling under the wall. The Warden, Henry Wirz required the Union prisoners to discipline their own men and was known to order Confederate guards to shoot prisoners for small infractions including the "dead line." (Wirz was hanged at Andersonville after the war for his crimes against prisoners).

Eugene described one poor boy who was killed by guards because he could not pull himself to the appropriate spot designated as the latrine area. Eugene wrote he "Determined that they shouldn't bury his bones in that place." He lost so much weight, he could wrap his hand around his leg just above the knee. He ate anything, including bugs and grass. He was so emaciated, he could barely walk and weighed around eighty pounds.

With great good fortune, the South became desperate for skilled workers toward the end of the war and Eugene was engaged to work for his captors as a blacksmith outside the walls. They gave him food and after a few weeks of recuperation,

Eugene became strong enough to work at his old trade. Within a few months, he was trusted by his captors and one night, he walked away from his shop and made a successful escape. He walked several hundred miles back to his beloved home in Lititz, Pennsylvania. In his memoirs, Eugene stated "neither tongue nor pen can describe the horrors of the war as experienced on the battlefield and in the prison pen."

Eugene ended his narrative by relating "In spite of those horrific experiences, he held malice toward none and charity toward all." He lived to raise a fine family and died in 1916.

About the Author

Dr. Zeiss was president of Pueblo Community College in Colorado and Central Piedmont Community College in Charlotte, North Carolina for a combined 32 years. He has authored 20 books in historical, educational, and self-improvement genres. He was named the 2005 CEO of the Year for all 1,200 community colleges in America by the Association of Community College Trustees. He was the founding Executive Director of the Museum of the Bible in Washington, D.C. 2017-18 and an educational consultant until 2022.